PARADOX

PARADOX

INCOGNITO

ATTENTION
<u>IMPORTANT NOTICE</u>

TAKE OFF YOUR MASKS BEFORE READING.

TAKE OFF YOUR MASKS BEFORE READING.

TAKE OFF YOUR MASKS BEFORE READING.

TAKE OFF YOUR MASKS BEFORE READING.

TAKE OFF YOUR MASKS BEFORE READING.

TAKE OFF YOUR MASKS BEFORE READING.

REMOVE.

OFF.

YOUR.

MASKS.

<u>they aren't welcomed</u>

INTRO

in some moments of your life, there are hidden thoughts that
question all the indoctrinations you've been conditioned into.
whether you can acknowledge it or not, you feel a slight
indication that everything you've been told is not what it
seems to be. these moments aren't coincidental because
you never create your thoughts; they just come to you,
like hiccups. like rain falling from a clear sky.

and maybe you come to the assumption that what you call
reality may just be an illusion. you then start to notice the
missing dots but haven't quite figured it out entirely yet so
by default, you stay in line. lost in the illusion until hopefully
one day it makes sense. but the fact of the matter is, as long as
you fall prey to the distractions, you'll be destined to stay in a
whirlpool of confusion because that's what the illusion does.
it's ingrained in your thinking patterns, tension span,
actions and feelings.

the insanity of this illusion is you're controlling it yourself.

its only leverages are persuasion, influence and temptation.

if you ignore the distractions, you'll begin to see there's

something sinister and intelligently constructed in this illusion.

before you list the hundreds of possibilities of

what this illusion could be, there's only one question to ask:

what is it that you feel when you say "I"?

you are the illusion

with no fault of your own, the illusion you are always looking

for is the one that stands before you in the mirror. i say with no

fault of your own because you've been dealt a bad hand.

someone gave you a name, religion, nationality and belief

system that became the personality you call yourself.

your experiences became you without knowing it's just a

character. your idea of yourself does not explain how the

organs in your body function, it does it on its own without

your conscious attention and yet, it manages for the most part.

you feel that what isn't in your control is not you.

the only way to escape this illusion is to take off your masks.

once you read this, you agree to have that mask taken off,
temporarily. even if you find yourself terrified, take them off.
they aren't needed here. why? because they don't exist.
they were never there to begin with.
you might not be the you, you think you are.

before we begin,
as you read throughout this story,
do not try to understand what i mean by my words.
think about what the words mean to you.
i left my words for you to fill your thoughts
and maybe even add some of your own.
don't think of good or bad
but rather what you want.
not about right or wrong
but rather what you feel.

enter

CONTENTS

BEHIND THE MASK

Persona /'pərˈsōnə/ n. 1. character
　　　　　　　　　　　　2. personality
　　　　　　　　　　　　3. mask

"at some point when you create yourself to make it,
you're going to have to either let that creation go and take
a chance on being loved or hated for who you really are,
or you're going to have to kill who you really are and fall into
your grave grasping onto a character that you never were."

-Jim Carrey

the mask you wore so long
you forgot you ever put it on.
an ego built from social institutions
created in your own self-image.
yet you think it's you and not separate.
but before your ego was created you were still you.
so, who were you before you were born?

the mask

when you figure out
what exactly it is you mean when you say "I",
you then have to ask yourself,
who is the one conscious of your "I"?
and until you wake up, you'll keep cutting off heads
of the snake just to see three more take its place.

the character created that you call "you" is a concept.
we identify ourselves with the role we play
and live believing these two are one.
what began as a gift eventually turned into a trap.
the "I" is just a collection of experiences
gathered together with conscious attention
to make a construct; an idea. an image of ourselves.
in modern day, our egos control us until
we're able to distinguish the difference.
to build the separation between the self and the ego,
be conscious of the thoughts that run in your head.
let it play and watch.
then ask who is it that is aware of the observer?

if you keep looking for yourself in your ego, you'll find
yourself creating more and more masks. it's only when you
look in yourself will you find that there's nothing to look for.
you're it.

the game of hide and seek

having an ego is not the problem,
believing you are the ego is.

we aren't aware of the masks we wear because
ideas and concepts are something
you can never see, touch or break.

by believing you're just an idea,
you distract yourself from what you really are.

we need mirrors to remind ourselves of the masks we put on.
without mirrors, we would only have our memories.
but memories are distorted.
memories can change the color
of a room, a smell and even a face.
but most times it becomes an interpretation
of what we really wanted them to be.

smoke and mirrors

we are all actors,
not characters themselves.

there's a reason you're always told
you can be anything you want to be

you see society differently
when you see the world as a stage;
when you realize we're all playing
our part so good it feels real.

in japan, fireflies are only visible in the night.
this keeps their beauty alive and appreciated.
you don't always have to be seen by everyone
or even yourself to know your worth.

you can never really know someone;
you only know what they show you.

people can change themselves, not their egos.
do you love yourself or your ego?

stop trying to find yourself in your
identity and just let go of all of it.
you can convince people of the mask you wear
but don't try to convince yourself.

self-love means being honest with yourself
even when the pill is too big to swallow.
ignoring the truth will only lead to more mess.
and after a while of being in a mess,
it's hard to remember where you came from,
even where you were going.

we wear masks because we know
with a mask on no one can truly hurt us.
but what is a fight without blood and sweat?
what is life without tears of pleasure and pain?

you are not separate from your environment.
everything around you is connected
like front and back and you couldn't
have a front unless you had a back.
you don't come into this world,
you grow out from it.
we love each other
for the same reasons we hate each other.
because somewhere in the
maze of someone else's identity,
we find bits and pieces of ourselves.

everything is complex
because of how simple it is.
life is simple.
we make it complex because if it weren't,
it would be complicated.

<u>overthinking the obvious</u>

PARADOX

we cover ourselves with material
to breathe life into our masks.
we feel the need to add more to ourselves
because we're terrified that without an ego,
we'll be invisible and lose touch with reality.
but we forget about the person
that wore the mask in the first place.

material cannot breathe.
it cannot talk or relate to you.
it has no life, no substance.
without our value of it,
it would be just as useless
as gold on a deserted island.

cry when getting rid of your ego
and laugh when you realize it never existed

everything makes more sense
when you stop trying to make sense of it

know by not knowing

being an old soul doesn't just mean
you're more mature and
wise than people around you.
it's being able to look at things outside yourself.
it's understanding that
some things can't be understood.
and being okay with that.

<u>confusion mixed with certainty</u>

other people are mirrors for knowing yourself;
every reaction.
every pro-action.
the more people you meet,
the more undiscovered qualities
you'll find about yourself.

through drugs we're able to access
thoughts and emotions that we normally don't feel
but drugs and love can only bring out those feelings,
they cannot place them there.

wanting a quality someone else has
means you already have it in you.
for you to want it,
you have it in yourself first.

we live in a day of age
where we find it hard to form intimate relationships.
we were raised watching life through
the television that gave us the choice
to watch life happen instead of
living though our own experiences.
we watch actors form those relationships for us
so we never have to deal with the humiliation
and rejection that comes with meeting new people.

we have phones to pull out in front of us
whenever we feel uncomfortable which
send a subconscious message to everyone else
that says:
"you're not as important to me right now."

we begin to watch emotion through our eyes
and forget to feel emotion with our eyes closed.

understand others
and you'll understand yourself

instead of bettering a community,
better yourself.
if everyone betters themselves,
you will create a community of better individuals.
then there will be nothing else left to do but to enjoy.

by taking care of yourself, you take care of others

the ones who are brave enough to lose themselves
will always find themselves.

you can't find something you haven't lost

being alone isn't bad.
being around people who make you feel lonely is.

will you sacrifice your ego
in return for your soul?

it can never be caught or attained.
you can only run after it until you exhaust yourself;
satisfaction is vanity.
there is no endless joy.
the closer you get,
the farther it is.
until you realize you'll never get it,
you'll always chase after it.
realize the time and energy
you waste running after something
that was never there to begin with.
never caught but always pursued.

the shadow

wanting to stay in a constate state of happiness
is what causes you to stay in a continuous state of torture

we often cause more pain because we want to be happy.
but what if you get rid of wanting
the opposite of something you have?
the weight that you've been carrying
with you your entire life falls.

the idea of permanence is the main cause of pain

we were taught that what we can't control is not us
which makes us feel separate from the external world.
we go on believing we have no relation to what is outside us
causing the need to hold on to things so they won't leave.

clinging to yourself or others would be like
holding in your breath so you never lose it.
but by holding it in, you lose it.
it's only when you let it go
are you able to get it right back.

the rabbit hole is meant to go deep deep down,
although it is infinite and never ending.
it's only when you realize that
will the rabbit hole transcend you
to the same place where you fell in,
but not as the same person.
just like the mountain is meant to climb
even though the other side is the
same ground from where you started.
the mountain is high and takes time to climb
to bring you where you already were, reborn.

this world will break you down until
you're on your last breath.
but the only thing it can't take
away from you is your faith.
not religion or hope but faith.
only you can give that away.

if you're always thinking of being somewhere you aren't,
you will never live in the present.
because when you get there,
you'll want to be somewhere else.

<u>daydreaming</u>

grow up
graduate school
find a job
raise a family
slowly fall in your grave regretting everything
because your entire life you've been looking for "happiness"
and for the first time you realize you had it in you all along.

the rat race

as kids we look up to older people
believing that they know everything.
it's not until we grow up that we realize
even the people we once looked up to
are still trying to figure it out.

when you're at your lowest point
and can't find strength,
give into the darkness
and there you will find the light.

no prison can ever compare
to the imprisonment of the mind.

<u>you're in search for a key</u>
<u>when there is no door or locks</u>

FALLACY OF WORDS
words: <u>an effort to explain the things that can't be explained</u>

the things that can't be explained are most divine.
writers know how to use their words
but words are just sound that describe abstractly.
the word love is only a drop of water
compared to what it really is.
what you call "you" is just one
of the many characters you decide to act as.

we think of words and actions as the highest quality
but nothing in this world can be
meaningful without the feeling.
it's feelings that give us a reason to live.
behind explanation is the unexplainable
tear dropping beauty of all.

the only reason we continue to live

the only things that are considered normal
are the concepts everyone has already agreed upon.
we never dared to question while we grew up,
we were told that this is how it is
and so we followed the routine.

walking barefoot in a dark room full of nails

technology has given us more masks
than any actor has ever had.
we think we're failures when we don't succeed for the
first time we try something due to instant gratification.
technology has given us the illusion
of the easy route; the easy and fake life.
these masks may be bulletproof but
they'll fall off easily when you start
to feel like the world is against you.
when you see not everything is as it seems,
you either throw your masks away to reach your limitless
or make more masks and break with them.

what do you do when you find that there is
nothing you can do and there is nothing
you cannot do to find yourself? you watch.
as if you were watching your own movie
but from a different point of view.
you become a mirror, reflecting what is in front of you but
never holding on to what is there. after a while of doing so, you
will start to see your existence for the first time; reborn with a
new state of awareness. there is nothing normal about anything
and there is no need to worry about anything.

i get lost in my head sometimes
tangled and stuck in my thoughts.
it took me years of trying to find a way
to outsmart myself to realize there is no me.

our thoughts rule our lives.
we have become addicted to our thoughts.
we feel the need to occupy ourselves
and think of more thoughts
to avoid the feeling of boredom;
to avoid being alone with ourselves.

you live in a big circus with bright lights
to distract you from the sun that lives within you.

sometimes knowing is a curse.
the need to explain everything
is a rabbit hole that doesn't end; it's vanity.
you can never know too much.
i always understood why
adam and eve bit the forbidden fruit,
now i understand why god tried to prevent it.

the knowing

what do you mean when you say i?
i don't think any question could be as interesting as that.
whether aliens exist or not couldn't
be as interesting as that because when you go
into the nature of what is oneself,
you begin to realize that "you"
have become an alien to yourself.

ENTER

LOVE

HATE

DESIRE

STUCK BETWEEN THE LINES
OF LUST AND HELL
JUST TO AVOID FALSE LOVE

the transition from normal
to something words can't describe;
falling in love will always
be better than being in love.

happy ever ~~after~~ now

when everything is perfect,
it's the wind before the storm.
enjoy these moments.

the fall

we didn't have to talk,
i already knew you without meeting you.

like thieves know thieves without introduction

the relationship you have with yourself
often represent the kind of relationship you have with others.

if you find yourself feeling
more scared to lose someone
than enjoying being with them,
it isn't love;
it's greed.

if you react while someone is talking,
you weren't listening; you were waiting to speak.
you don't want to talk; you want to argue.

a toxic relationship can turn lips that
once felt soft to broken glass.
i went from loving to see you smile
to smiling when you cried.
i did love you.
but i also loved seeing you hurt.

i was the main cause of your pain,
i can admit that now.

*tears running down our face
when we realize we're not for each other*

what they don't tell you about love is
sometimes the person you want to protect
is the same person you're hurting.

you're always saying my happiness comes first,
that you want me to be happy.
you told me it was okay to want my own joy
but it's not.
not if my heaven is your hell.

it's not that i hated you,
i hated myself
and hurt people will hurt people.
i left you not because i have a problem with you
but because i have a problem with myself.
most times you are your own worst enemy

<u>devil in disguise</u>

with you my mind was empty.
now my mind feels like a room of memories,
filled without an empty spot.

how can someone be sad
and happy at the same time?
in awe that you can cherish memories
but terrified of the thought that everything
from those memories will one day fade
as if they never happened.

the illusion of time will push you
further from the present

if you find yourself always looking for love in the wrong places, it's your body telling you to find love within yourself.

it's reassuring when you find people who only want sex
but after nights and nights with different people,
all the faces start to cluster together
only to forget whose bed you're in
while the same old song starts to play again.

desire with no love

now i can barely remember a face.
only the moments of passionless lust love
and lovers that i destroyed

*if you enjoy love
you must learn to accept pain*

we praise one but couldn't feel
either unless you had the other

love/hate

we'll always love each other
because we never stay long.
every time we meet
it feels like the first time.

i like these moments with you
because we never get used to each other

i like the idea of you so i never want to meet you
(you like the idea of them but
can you accept their demons?)

stuck with a fantasy because there it can never be ruined.
don't wrap your mind around the idea of love
because one day when you're loved how you
felt you needed to be, you won't be able to sleep
after finally realizing that even after
getting everything you wanted,
it's still not enough to satisfy you.

the unpleasant surprise of desire

society lost the meaning of love
by confusing love with obligation.
love is not a duty.
love is not responsibility.
when you love you do it out of joy;
not because you are expected or obligated to.
you confuse love for slavery when doing so.

you can try to fake your identity
but you can't fake your feelings.

you can still be selflessly selfish.
doing good for your own satisfaction
doesn't make you a good person.
being genuine means doing good
for the same reason trees grow and the sky rains.

if you obey your religion or relationship but don't agree,
it would be the same as doing the complete opposite.
you're lying to yourself.
to be honest is to do what you feel
despite if it's wrong or someone gets hurt.
you shouldn't be forced to
do something you disagree with,
even telling someone you love
them when you don't.
why pretend your feelings
are other than what they are?
your feelings aren't ever wrong because
you don't force them, they just come to you.
if you believe your feelings are wrong,
you don't need to change your feelings,
you need to change yourself.

if two people are arguing,
they both are right and wrong.
we usually speak through experience
not knowing we all are right in our own way.
learn how to speak without being bias.
learn how to discuss instead of trying to be right.

hatred doesn't always lead to violence and disagreement,
unacknowledged hatred does.
don't deny yourself from feeling what you feel,
your feelings will only overflow making more of a mess.
don't try to hide what you feel.
be aware of what's bothering you and be okay with it.
but once you begin to find yourself in other people,
it'll be harder for you to get mad at anyone
because you understand them so well.

not telling someone you've fallen
out of love with them isn't heroic;
it's a dirty secret heavier than
any burden you've ever carried before.

it's not that you don't want to hurt them
but rather how much pain you'll feel when you come
face to face with the fact that you've been trying
to recreate a memory you can't help letting go of.

you found something you
never knew existed and believe by letting go
you're leaving the one thing that
drugs and pleasures could never compare to;
that you just might fall back
into the lifeless bottom pit of nothing.

something worth dying for

|die|sire

you suffer because you desire.
you hold onto a rose despite of its thorns
but a rose will never be as alive as it is in the soil.
there are repercussions to desire.

let go.
this is something you don't try to do, you just do.
don't try to let go because then
you'll be desiring not to desire.
when you really want to stop the pain,
you'll let go of the rose with 100 thorns
just to see 1000 roses grow around your feet.

know when to leave.
even the most gorgeous flowers die.
know when the love has died.
when one love dies,
thousands of more grow.
appreciate what you had
instead of trying to relive a memory.

whether it's a lover or even yourself

most of us don't understand what trust is.
some people can only trust if
there is certainty or reassurance.
trust is not knowing whether or not the outcome
you want will happen while still having faith
that it will go the way you want it to.
we lack the ability to trust because we fear being hurt
but not trusting is what causes more frustration.

i'm not mad you said we wouldn't last,
i'm mad we didn't try.
you're the reason i left
but i'm the reason you didn't stay.

what's the point of watering a dead flower?

if you hate someone you once loved,
don't say you loved them.
if you say you love someone
you care for their happiness,
not possessing them.

we wear our hearts on our sleeves
   only to bring out our horns
   after having those sleeves
   torn apart piece by piece.

you want people to admire your exterior
because the last time you showed someone
your true self they destroyed you.
but the consequence of love is
one moment of love
for a year of pain.
but even then, it's still worth it.

when you want to be loved you will
be balancing on a rope between two mountains.
it's only when you love without expectation
that you jump off the tightrope with a smile.

love without expecting and you will never be dissatisfied

the worst sin is when you knew your options
and still picked the worse one.

i was never scared to share my thoughts,
i just wasn't ready to admit them.

i'd rather hurt you than
be the reason you can't fall in love again.
even if i'm forced to miss you every day.

lesser of two evils

i let you go not because i didn't like you
but because i loved you.

stop looking for someone to
take care of your loneliness.
learn how to be okay with being alone.
being social should be an option,
not a necessity.

PARADOX

you gave me meaning
when i needed wholeness

i know what love is until you ask me.
you're asking for words when love is a feeling.

the brain will never understand the heart

love is the abandonment of logic;
the relinquishment of everything that makes sense.

i put too much of my pride aside and died shy

too much of anything will kill you

if your heart is worn out
find a reason to get back.
the breaking
the healing
the disappointment
these are the reasons why love makes perfect.
we choose to be burnt by the fire
because what else is there to do
in a cold room filled with gas and matches?
it's the fire that reminds us
how only through pain will we find bliss.
and it's always warm before it starts to burn.

everyone should experience
a heartbreak because without it,
life would be a like a
rollercoaster without twists and turns.

we either hurt when in love
or feel the pain of walking away from love

don't love their character, love their imperfections
no one is perfect.
but maybe you can find if
you're perfect for each other.

you know you found someone who really cares
when they love seeing your eyes fill up with light
while you talk about the things your passionate about.

sex is overrated.
passion mixed with love will have you weak.

money is overrated.
turning work into play will turn everyday into friday.

tell me what runs through your mind.
the things that keep you up at night.
the things you felt no one would understand.

seduction

love is an emotional connection.
compatibility is a logical connection.
these two are oil and water;
<u>the double ended blade.</u>
to love someone completely
is to love them how you love yourself.
it's to do what is best for that person and
sometimes what's best for the one you love
may not always involve you.
real love won't regret letting go
but rather appreciate the times you had together.

let's not put any conditions on us.
can we just enjoy each other and be okay with that?

from me, to you

i left you because i needed you to love yourself before you
even considered loving me, but you ended up burying
yourself in a hole, broken. dying of loneliness and sadness
until someone else would carry you out. it breaks me that you
think i was finished with you; i was waiting for you.
and now i'm one of the bad on your naughty list
that destroyed you. i wonder if you'll ever find the light
i wanted to show you or if i'd even tell you. seeing you
happy in your little bubble you call love, that isn't love.
you can't love someone else if you can't love yourself.
sadly, i still have a small part of me waiting for you but
another part of me happy that you found your own peace.
regardless if it's an illusion or not,
i just really enjoy seeing you smile.

no one can pull you out of a dream
until you decide to wake up yourself.

i feel like we said "maybe in the next life" in our past lives.
let's share a moment in this life where we didn't say that.
a moment that wouldn't matter
if we remember it or not in our next life.

i can offer more than love.
i'll always be there for you even
if you won't be there for me.
even though i'm not the one you end up with,
i'll keep you on your feet when it feels like
the whole world is pushing you down.

if you leave,
the door is open for you to walk out
and come back as you please.
i know this isn't about us.
it's about us individually and
we don't have to be close to love each other
because i don't just love you
i unconditionally have love for you.
i never wanted you,
i wanted your happiness.
we may be in love but we both have our own paths
and i understand that.
and i'm okay with that.

if you were once friends
you will always be friends
because friends never say goodbye.
even without labels to connect them to one another.
even if time apart from each other turns permanent.

a missed connection with someone you just met
can hurt so much that you feel it physically.
a rejection will never be as bad as watching the person
who could've changed your life completely walk away.
not knowing if you'll ever meet each other again
or just become a ghost of the past.

every close encounter is a story waiting to be told

you wouldn't know you were good
if there weren't any bad people.
love your enemies.
because not only do you need them
but without them,
you wouldn't know what you stand for.

if you can't find the good in others
how can you use the good in you?
if you can't find the bad in yourself
how can you help others?

once you see you create your ego
in the same way you create good situations from bad ones
and bad situations from good ones, being a person doesn't
seem like life or death but rather a game to be experienced.
simply to enjoy what's here and now.
and if your mask begins to feel heavy, you remember that
it's just a role; that you don't have to hold on so tight,
when looking through your eyes,
it's normal to believe you are a person.
but if you can change your perception
and look at your world from a larger point of view,
you'll see that you are part of a larger self.
this is just as true for identities
as it is for relationships.

THE DEATH OF THE EGO

there's no such thing as being happy or sad forever.
feelings come in waves that arrive differently every crash.

ENTER HERE

LIFE IN THE

RABBIT HOLE

we want what we desire until
we realize we don't know what we want.
....
the burden of knowing
is the absence of a spontaneous surprise

the devil isn't red
with horns and a pitchfork.
the devil is everything you want;
not knowing what you wish for,
you already possess.

child's play

we decorate our bad memories
because no one wants a garden with dead flowers

pain is inevitable.
the only way to stop the pain is to enjoy it;
embrace pain to find bliss.

worrying is a parasite in your head,
of all the infinite possibilities of happenings,
chooses the worst.

an illusion of fearing to be burned
without a fire to even do so.

what disturbs you more?
the thought of nothing being after death?
or that you don't know?

<u>TIME</u>

an illusion used to keep you focused
on the past and future but never in the now.
the only thing you can ever be
certain about is the eternal now.
the past is just a memory.
the future is imaginary.
we use cause and effect to justify our actions.
we separate events and forget that it's
all one continuous event divided into sections.
in the real world, there are no separate events.

it's only when times are hard
do we feel time slow down.
only when we're happy does time start to speed.
when our life is perfect it wasn't long enough;
when our life is not what we wanted it
to be is when we feel eternal agony.

the ones that accept death
are usually the ones that live longer

GOD'S TRIP

"suppose every night you could dream any dream you
wanted to dream and have the power within one night
to dream seventy-five years of time or any other length you
wanted to have. naturally on this adventure, you would fulfill
all your wishes. you would have every kind of pleasure. and
after several nights of seventy-five years of pleasure each,
you get an exciting idea of having a dream which isn't
under control. where something is going to happen to you
but you don't know what's it going to be.
and finally, after doing that for a while,
you would dream the life you are living right now.
the dream of playing that you weren't god."

-Alan Watts

you never know you're dreaming until you wake up.
maybe you're locked in dreams of dreams
and reality is what you want it to be.
it's only when you wake up that you realize
you wasted a dream by thinking it was real.

to the ones that feel undeserving,
the ones that drowned when
the storm was too much to handle,
the ones taunted and controlled by their demons,

enjoy this dream.
you won't remember it when you wake up.

COGNITIVE DISSONANCE

what is like to go to sleep and never wake up?
after thinking about that for some time
another question comes which is
what was it like to wake up after never gone to sleep?
these are questions that we avoid every day
because we hate the feeling of not knowing.
the fear that there's nothing for us after death,
that we'll float endlessly in nothing and darkness.
why worry about death while living?
why worry about tomorrow and ruin today?
why would we be born if we're
all destined to be doomed to nothingness?
why would the sun go down if it wouldn't come back up?
maybe for the same reason we love someone and let them go.
to go on living forever would be boresome.
we learn to love when we lose what we love,
it's the only thing that gives love true meaning;
when we pass off the torch to someone
who hasn't had that beautiful burning fire.

if you know that you are everything,
then you should know that death isn't the end of the show.

the rabbit hole of a broken heart

you will have those dark moments
when you lay in bed,
thinking of the life you want.
not knowing how it will come or when,
but you're left with a vision you desire badly.
when all you feel is sadness and lost hope.
dry crying because you're empty.
because you lost the ability
of out running your fears
and finally, they've caught up to
you. so, you lay there.
stuck in a field of confusion waiting
for a miracle to come but it doesn't.
it's at that time something awakens
which will change you forever.
you become hungry enough for that vision
that you will run through hell for it,
whether you deserve it or not.
you decide to fight for it because
you're tired of waiting for a miracle.
you take things in your own hands
and that's when you become the miracle
you've waited for your whole life.
or you decide to let your dreams
play in your head and they die with you.

PARADOX

you grow up believing your superheroes
will come to help you when you're in trouble.
it's only when no one comes
do you become fully aware
that if you do not save yourself,
you will turn into what you always feared.

when you want something
more than you want life,
that's when it happens.
die for what you love
and you'll survive.

<u>self-sacrifice</u>

if you don't like where you are in your life,
it's because you live in the future, not the present.
if you have no future to compare your present to,
you will learn how to be fully in the present; in the now.

learn how to appreciate what's here now
and what you want will present itself to you.

fear the feeling of fear.
if anything should scare you,
it should be the feeling of fear
and that will make you courageous

fighting fear isn't an overnight project,
it isn't something you leave behind you.
all emotions and thoughts are stained
on you like a birthmark.
what makes fear important
isn't jumping off the cliff into the
unknown without care or hesitation,
the importance of fear is to fearfully jump into
the unknown without knowing what will happen.
without fear there is no meaning of bravery.
bravery is being scared shitless,
yet walking into the eye of the storm.
you learn to live without listening to fear.
because it isn't a fight,
it's a dance.
to become god, you must first live as man.

now i have to help the ones who beat me.
the ones that were too cheap
and chose money over me.
who left me alone when i couldn't eat.
the ones that cursed me and
wouldn't give me water when i was thirsty.

hard pills to swallow

it took me years to realize it wasn't
that i couldn't see what others could
but that i see what they ignore.

not remembering where we were
before birth is like restarting a game.
the game is not to be won or lost
but to be enjoyed.

love for knowledge will bring you to insanity.
love not for knowledge
but for being.
not for wisdom
but to experience.
not to understand but to feel.

putting what you feel into words
will distract you from the feeling itself. you
begin to think instead of feel.
by trying to understand what love is you will
never understand it.

if you spend your time thinking,
you will live a life of your own in your head.
if you think about life
you will miss it.
live your life
and you will understand it.

Avidyā

(sanskrit for ignorance)

as you embrace life,
you must embrace death in the same manner.
they're non-dual.
you couldn't have one without the other.
like a coin has two sides; heads and tails.
you couldn't just have one side
or it wouldn't be a coin.
black implies white, death implies life,
bad implies good, self implies other.
separate but still one.
individual but need each other to exist.

CONTROL pt.1

your need for control is the reason
why nothing is going your way.
learn to be okay with not knowing
or learn to live in hell on earth.

CONTROL pt.2

man has always strived for control and dominance which has
been great for the short run but damaging in the long run.
when will we realize the universe is too smart for us?
when will we realize simplifying will only complicate?

the cost of knowing that you're happy
is knowing that you're sad

you either follow your soul
and do what you're passionate about
or sell your soul doing what you're told
and never loving what you do.

spiritual suicide

it's not worth living a life you don't want to live
when your soul is on a completely different path.
you may be able to ignore your passions and goals
but your soul will leave you to follow them faithfully.

one day
you will break down to your lowest point
because these masks aren't made
to survive during hard times.
and when you feel broken,
close your eyes for a second and realize
hell isn't a place filled with fire and evil;
hell is a state of mind.

this world is run by events, not things.
continuous happenings that are
ruled by what kind of attitude
you want to take to the world.

before i lost feeling,
i could never tell which would be worse;
to feel or to have never felt at all.
but when you fall into nothingness,
no joy, no pain
no love, no hate
no fear, no light
no shame, no grief
just an empty black hole.
numb, nothing and alone.
an ocean of nonexistence.
empty. soulless.
now i know i would rather be tortured in
hell than to have never felt anything at all.

why do we have a need for religion?
maybe for the same reason we have the need for belief.
but to believe in something ultimately means
we. do. not. know.
and that really bothers us.
so we decide to cling onto a belief that will reassure us
that there's something to look forward to.
which it will, until you start to question it
and find yourself jumping from one belief to another.
if you'd like to know,
stop looking everywhere for it
and start looking inside you.

maybe we should all take a break
from religion and belief.
if it's there now, it'll be there later.
a break from being told
what to think
what to feel
what to wear
what to eat
stop caring for a moment
and you'll feel the breeze of freedom.
that breeze will blow the sand from your eyes
to show you the world you live in

we are all programmed,
whether by religion, society or emotion.
i will not give you another belief to cling onto
but rather remove the foundation
of conditionings beneath you.
and where you land will be your choice;
if you decide to land.

we confuse
status with improvement
weakness with kindness
lust with love
ignorance with confidence
possession with fulfillment
job promotions with happiness
wealth with money
masks with ourselves

welcome to the human race

we spend all our time worrying about things
that distract us from the obvious
and rarely have alone time for ourselves.
we spend all our time on the run for so long
alone time becomes a frightening thought.
and the only thing that really
scares us is the thought of being alone;
the thought of not being on the run.
because after doing something for so long
it becomes a habit, a stain.
like a tattoo signature on our bodies;
an open wound that never heals

it's only when you observe yourself
will realize you have been living
in a dream house of illusions your entire life
made for you to feel like you don't deserve
what you were born with;
freedom

find what makes you uncomfortable, what makes you cringe.
go outside your comfort zone and there is the truth,
the only thing you can't run from.

if you keep looking in the same direction,
stop expecting to see a different image.
it's only when you open yourself to see
new directions, will you see something different.
you'll eventually be able to see all directions
when you stop sticking to one way of viewing.

the one who is always thinking,
will have nothing to think about
but thoughts and noise.

intelligent stupidity

if we keep teaching our generation
how to find a well-paid job rather than
encouraging them to follow their passion,
we will eventually replace humanity
with machines that do what they're told.
teach others how to think
not what to think.

it takes money to keep a living
but it takes passion to be alive

the quickest way to learn
is to forget what you know.
the only way to gather more information
is to become empty like you were as a child.

it's ironic how we can see the wrongs in history
but never the wrongs in the present.
how we can see the faults in other groups
but never our own.

would you let your children leave
if you knew it would make them happy?
would you let her go if you're
the one who isn't growing up?
would you let him grow if
you're the one holding him down?

confused between appreciation and possession

i dare you to break the cycle;
the cycle of being machinery.
the cycle of going to work doing
something you have no relation with.
break the cycle.
what makes you itch?
what is it that you love to do?
what makes you cry and smile?
what keeps you up day and night?
money does not rule you.
ignore what you know
and fight for what you love.
run through hell with a smile
because you are the very
root and structure of existence itself
and only you can choose to settle for less.

only if you dare

once you see that everything right is wrong,
what is right and what is wrong are just imaginary,
you come to the realization that what you thought
you knew is just an ounce of what actually is.
when the curtain of illusion is taken off
it can leave you in an unfamiliar space.

we regret the things we didn't know
more than the things we consciously ignored

CONTRADICTIONS

we love yet we hate. we laugh yet we cry.
we ourselves are contradictions.
we want what we don't have.
if you spend all your time trying to
make sense of it, you'll die insane.
this is something that cannot be logically explained
but still makes sense.
and that's the beauty of it.

i found myself asking more questions without any answers
but the things we can't explain eventually bring clarity.

ENTER

RENAISSANCE

"get the most emotion from every emotion;
after maximum pain, comes maximum happiness"

i stopped running away from my demons
and made friends with them

the dopamine we get
from technology have turned us into addicts.
we turn to social media and other distractions
for refuge when we feel stressed and depressed
just to avoid dealing with what's really bothering us.
we don't have the coping mechanism
to confront our demons. instead we let them
ride our backs until we find new distractions
to save us from our own state of mind.

life is not easy;
never has been, never will be.
the truth of the matter is the people
who live their lives joyfully know this.
they know life can be a tornado of disaster
and the only way of experiencing it is
to stop resisting it and just dance with it.
with your eyes closed go with the flow of it.
because once you decide to stop resisting
the current of the river, it will help you move faster.

the dance

thinking positively won't always
take you where you want to go
but it'll give you a positive way
to look at negative situations,
so you have the strength
to change them in the most productive way.

risk chasing your dreams.
that doesn't mean you're never going to fail,
but any pain that you feel
will never compare to the regret
that comes with walking away
from what you love.

passion

the only way to find peace is to stop looking for it
why look for something you already have?

i am knowingly selfish.
maybe not in the conventional sense
but i am.
when you see that everything other than you
is a part of you and that there is no separation,
there really isn't any other choice.
to be truly in love with yourself
is to love what is outside of you
because there is no inside without an outside.
and no outside without an inside.
that's the real meaning of being selfish;
helping others as if you were helping yourself.
the more you give,
the more you get back.

don't tell me what's best for me
let me go my way and walk with me
maybe then you can see what i see

someone else's advice may not work for you.
they are giving the advice from their experience.
make a choice from your own advice.
if you fail, learn
and if you learn, you will always win

the hardest part about giving advice is taking your own

it's not your fault you've
landed in any given situation.
bad can happen to anyone anywhere
but it is your responsibility to change it.
you can either take charge of your life
or learn to accept it.

responsibility over fault

"god became man so that
man might become god."

(anthanasius of alexandria)

try to be better, not the best;
you can only lose if you were trying to win

your intuition will have a mind of its own
when you stop thinking about how you feel
and start acting on what you feel

all the inventions we have access to
seemed impossible at one point of time.
being realistic will keep you in line.
being unrealistic creates the future.

often the life we live was chosen
because it was the easy path
disguised as being "realistic."
we fear not being able to achieve
what we really want to do so
we play the role given to us.
we decide to live a life doing
something we have no true interest in.

no one knows exactly where impulses come from.
the question shouldn't be where they come from
but whether you decide to act on them or not.
your impulses are attracted to your character.

if you are going to do something,
good or bad, do it all the way.
if you decide to do bad,
continue through with the act.
decide what side of the fence you want to be on.
if you lie, then finish through with the lie.
if you start a project, finish it.
don't hesitate.
hesitating will only lead to more guilt
because if you lie and get caught in a lie,
you'll then begin to start to lie to yourself.

lost between roads you have no memory of crossing.
and guilt will lead you to find different pleasures
to distract your mind instead of dealing with
how it all started in the first place.

improving the one who's doing the improvement

live lively
and your lungs will keep you alive
when life drags you down to
the bottom of the sea

galloping and laughing through hell

make a promise to yourself;
not me or your god.
not your parents or your peers.
but to yourself.
make a promise to yourself that this life
will not be one you regret;
to write your own story
even when you run out of ink.

destroy your belief system.
you don't need a god or a devil;
all you need is yourself.
pure consciousness.
find yourself by removing everything you know.

the sculptor

the focus should not be heaven or hell,
the focus should be here and now.
when you're dead you won't have anything
to be worried about because there
will be no one to be able to do the worrying.

most of us live life postponing death
rather than living life that was given to us.

you have no idea how you beat your own heart,
how you breathe without thought,
how you function your own body,
or how you manage to be conscious.
but the things you are not in control of flow perfectly.

i used to think that conquering the world
by your own power and having people
who obey you was the best thing in the world,
but now i'm certain that the person with the
most power is the one who has the ability to rule
but decides to walk away.

we're always told we have the power
to do whatever it is we want in life
but often we only imagine our power
as we walk away from what we really wanted.

your actions are aligned with your beliefs.
you get what you want
when you have the feeling
that you already have it.

we live for distraction to delay the question
we all eventually must ask ourselves which is:
"what do i want?"
and it's okay not to know.
what you really want is already known.
the key isn't to find the answer
but rather to keep momentum going.
learn more, grow more and
the answer will find you.

you won't find it because you already have it

do not limit yourself to what your eyes can see.
you may not be where you want to be
but if you can imagine the life you want
then it's yours to have.

knowledge will help your intuition,
but imagination can take you farther
than your intelligence ever will

(life)

when you breathe, inhale like it's your last;
just as you do when you
come out of water for air.
notice how easy it is to let go
and hard to keep in.

when you cry, rain.
cry out like a child when it doesn't get its way.
let your heart ache and nose run.
let everything out.

when you lay in the sun,
feel the sun's fire burn into your skin.
notice how powerful one star alone can be.
touch the grass.
let it stab you and peel your skin.

when you listen to your favorite song,
let it play as loud as it can.
scream it, sing the song to the song.

(continue)

and when you love, love.
lock up your mind and
pour yourself into someone.
jump off the cliff even if you know
no one will be there to catch you.
feel the attraction. feel them.
don't let your love live in absence.

you are human
you have the power of light and dark.
you are the root of existence.
you have the love of humanity in your soul.
these feelings you have are
the closest thing to reality.
it is not a fantasy.

you are a gift grown out the world. you
are small yet universes live inside you.
you think too much and feel too little.
without these qualities you are not alive
and if you aren't alive,
what else is there for you to be?

you can either listen to your head or your heart.
the heart is a road that lies where it so chooses
and the mind is a butterfly that goes
one place to another continuously
looking for a comfortable place to lie still.
the soul is emptiness without beginning;
choose to live carelessly or die carefully.

there is no beginning or end.
there's just the eternal now.
don't live for tomorrow, live for right now
because tomorrow never comes.
nothing around you matters except human connection.
the people you touch and love are
the only things you will leave on this beautiful mess.

the more you don't understand something
the closer you are to finding it out.

we all have faith,
whether we're aware of it or not.
whether it's religious, spiritual
or even through existence itself.
we plan out our days as if
we're promised tomorrow.
we walk confidently without thinking
of the possibility of the floor caving in under our feet.
we are not promised anything but by going through the
motions without a thought of something going wrong
does this kind of faith becomes virtuous.

you are a product of your environment.
you are all conditioned under certain dogmas
whether you can admit it or not, but you decide how much.
the only way to break through the cage
is to acknowledge your programming.
use your mind. use critical thinking.
question everything and do the research yourself.
to walk freely, you must first break your chains.

have faith without any
evidence that what you want is possible.
those who can have faith without
any evidence will always get what they want.

if you have yet to find what you love
and are dying to know do this:
lock yourself in your closet
without entertainment or distractions
and don't leave the room until you
find whatever it is you're looking for.
when you want to find what you really want
like a prisoner wants freedom,
then you will find that the answer is
the one thing you ignored all along.

who am i to determine
what's good or bad for someone?
you could win the lottery ticket and get hit by a car.
you can get evicted from your home and
get everything you ever wanted.
these events aren't logical,
they just happen from other happenings.
the best way to live is the way without a way.

in the gift wrapping could be a dead dog or diamonds.
it's the excitement of not knowing what's in the gift
that makes us want to open it, not the gift themselves.

there is no right or wrong,
only the ones given to us that we've accepted.
doing something good for someone
or even ourselves, can be disastrous.
we do what we believe is good to others because we feel
through our experience, it will be beneficial for them.
this can either scare you
or give you the strength to have faith that what
you do will somehow lead to something good.

there needs to be two opposing sides to a game.
without a game, there would be nothing to play.

what's the point of continuing a game
when you already know the outcome?
win or lose,
the simple fact that we don't know what is next
is the reason why we continue to play.

the only thing there is to understand
is that there is nothing to understand but to enjoy

there is no right answer as to
where you locate your i but
depending where you identify yourself
can limit you to certain heights.

be careful what you wish for.
you may get everything you asked for but
you can never take all data into consideration.
good could come from bad.
bad could come from good.
but to have the perseverance
to stick with what you want
will always be beneficial.
if things turn bad, you're learning.
if things lead to good, then you're enjoying.
and if you die, you won't remember it.

don't be afraid of not having a moral guide.
right could lead to wrong in the
same way wrong could lead to right.
you can never think everything through
but be aware of what you do.

i have no right to tell you what kind of life to live
but it's only fair that i show you your choices.
you may not be able to control what happens to you
but you can decide how you respond toward it.
you can either have love or hate,
choose one.
reality is what we choose it to be.
because in the end there is no reality.

it's better to be laughed at for doing what you love
than to have what you love die with you.

as we grew up,
we became too aware of ourselves.
we started to act as if we were our bodies
but there was a point of time when
we didn't think about this.
as children,
we did what we felt without hesitation.
we lost the ability to ride with the wind;
the oceanic feeling of wholeness.
we got in the way of ourselves.
it's only after the teachings
from our parents and environment
did we start to second guess ourselves.

decide how you want to define your reality.
someone's concept of life is their philosophical idea.
whether it's a pessimistic or optimistic view,
whether it's a religious or spiritual view,
these are someone's idea of how to perceive the world.
whatever kind of view you decide to take on life is right.
just because someone else's idea makes sense to you
doesn't mean you have to live in their world.
you are what you choose to be.
and although you cannot control what is,
you can decide how to act and react
to the world around and in you.

there are some of us who have ignored
the signs and feelings of something not being right.
there are some people who have developed
a tolerance for these kinds of questioning and
have followed the life that was designed for them.
the dreams they once had was thrown
behind them to continue this imprisonment.
after facing the obstacles of life, it wore them down.
and eventually they gave into the temptation
of being enslaved by a mask.
these people may be the people you love most.
and the ugly truth is when you decide to
leave this life of black and white for a life of passion,
they'll be the first ones to put you down.
they tell you to think more "realistically."
and sometimes the people you're doing it for
are the same ones who put you down.

there no such thing as a realistic view of life.
there are just some people who have lost
the imagination they had as a child.

while on your journey,
you are going to lose and add pieces to yourself.
and sadly, some of the pieces you lose
are the same ones holding you together.

the game

if you find yourself not wanting to remove your mask
because in your heart you believe that who you are is you,
and that there is no mask to remove, you already have.
and you don't even remember it happening.
the human race plays a game of:
"think about not thinking to stop thinking."
"who are you?"
"who do what to be when you're older?"
"do this only if you do it as if it was not asked of you."
"you must love me"
"you must be you"
"you must"
"you should"
"you shall"
"you"
as kids we have no way of defending ourselves from the
systems of the game. we are told to alter our feelings,
as if we have any control of that and since we know we cannot
control our feeling, a mask is created in order to attract the
proper way to act as a civilized member of society;
we became our own prisoners.

you are told
what you should do
what you have to do
what you cannot do
what is and what isn't acceptable.
the same game that keeps the regulars going to the bar.
the same game that causes depression, anxiety,
guilt, and disappointment.
the same game that keeps you on the
treadmill of constant movement, mentally and physically.
the same game that keeps us running from our own shadows.
the game that stitches masks to our face
with a warm needle along with locks and chains.
the joke we all go along with.
the game no one ever wins or lose.
the illusion passed on from our past generations to us.
so, we live finding a way to accept that we have become
our own shadows. we have become the illusion.
the illusion of being a "person"

the frustration of the double bind

my last message for you, the reader.

we often feel stuck. imprisoned.
in our bodies but more importantly our own minds.
a place we created for ourselves that once felt like home but
has now turned into a prison we cannot see, feel or escape.
we've been locked in our prison cells for so long
that we've forgotten when or how it was even built.
we designed a complex system in our mind
where every door leads to five more.
where darkness follows us even through walls
and eventually cover every corner.
trapped. in a body of skin and flesh.
trapped. in the mazes of our minds.
we find everything we can to decorate
this prison to make it more tolerable.
we may even let people in
because the lonesome can
eventually get heavy but most times
we keep people out to protect them
from what the darkness has created.
but every now and then, the thought comes back
to escape our cells.
to escape ourselves.

(continue)

so, we try to escape.
we turn to our daily hobbies, technology, sex, food,
drugs, materialism, and other pleasures that give us
the dopamine we're always searching for;
to repress the thought of being a chess piece of life.
to save us from ourselves.
as time goes on,
we find that those pleasures don't give the same
intensity of gratification as it used to.
we then turn to self-improvement.
we realize that nothing physically can save us,
so the key could be spiritual.
maybe we can find peace through the metaphysical
and if we cannot find it through our own power
then it can be given to us through religion.
but the darkness always finds
a way back to where it was created.
the thought of everlasting happiness becomes
a fantasy and slowly begins to fade.
what then? back to our old routine of usual pleasures?
you will continue to crawl through thousands of paths
just for them to lead you back to another to follow.
the question soon changes from
what should i do, to what can i do?

(continue)

it's not until you get everything you want
will you discover that your wants
aren't the key to getting rid of your pain.
this kind of desire does not lead to completion
but rather emptiness; a hollow shell.
we look for something powerful enough
to fill the hole of satisfaction
but even if you were to get that,
you will still find a reason as to why it isn't enough.

because life is not something to be conquered.
it is not a treasure hunt. you cannot lose or win at life.
the point is not to run to the finish line
but to enjoy it while it's running.
it's the beauty of the view while you ride.
not having to worry about what happens next
but rather what is happening now
and how you decide to act and perceive situations.
we live in a world of our own that we
forget that we are in and apart of the cosmos itself.

(continue)

you will go through the dilemma of vanity because
you are always searching for what you could have
and not seeing what you already possess.
you go through this maze because
you don't know who you really are.
what you're looking for, you already have.
it's knowing that you are already complete.
desire to experience,
not for a reason to push the darkness behind you.
darkness is the absence of light.
the light in you.
and the darkness in you.
the feeling of emptiness comes
when you try to bend everything to your will.
love while you experience life.
instead of mourning when these experiences are gone,
smile that you were able to feel the rush of happiness.
out of all the infinite possibilities, you are alive.
out of the nothingness, you came into existence.
we take the little things for granted
and never really see the beauty of it.
life has emerged for and from us.
we pay too much attention to the distractions that we forget
the power of existence. the power that brought us here.
and that power is you. you create life.

(continue)

love and hate will always be here.
light and dark complement each other.
when you love, be fully into the moment.
when hate comes, learn. be understanding.
look at things in the best way possible
because time grows the things it kills.
but life never ends.
a new beginning of another end.
a beginning and end that we are
aware of only in the present.
the present;
the only gift that will never expire.

the bite of the forbidden fruit

i love you no matter who you choose to be.
i may not know what role you play but you.
because there is no you or me.
we're a part of something more.
and whatever you decide to call this,
make the best of it.

namaste

out of the night that covers me,
black as the pit from pole to pole,
i thank whatever gods may be
for my unconquerable soul.

in the fell clutch of circumstance
i have not winced nor cried aloud.
under the bludgeonings of chance
my head is bloody but unbowed.

beyond this place of wraith and tears
looms but the horrors of the shade,
and yet the menace of the years
finds and shall find me unafraid.

it matters not how strait the gate,
how charged with punishments the scroll,
i am the master of my fate.
i am the captain of my soul.

-william ernest henley

ACKNOWLEDGMENTS

alan watts
carl jung
charles bukowski
dalai lama
denzel washington
eckhart tolle
friedrich nietzsche
hina hashmi
jiddu krishnamurti
jim carrey
johnny depp
keanu reeves
lao tzu
les brown
ma anand sheela
morgan freeman
osho
robert anton wilson
rupi kaur
siddhartha gautama
tao te ching
will smith

////////////////preview of next book////////////////

tell me how it felt.
you met me at a very strange time in my life.
i destroyed you to see if i could feel something;
guilt, remorse, regret, anything.
i didn't cry because i hurt you
but *because i felt nothing;*

WORKINGS OF A MASOCHIST

VOL. II

AUTHOR'S NOTES

this story has no chapters as books would normally have.
the pages in this book has no specific order and the names of
the chapters are not meant to summarize the meaning of the
section but rather the different stages you may go through
during and after reading the novel.
i do not want to create a new religion for you.
the point is to destroy your religions and masks,
to have absolutely nothing to cling onto.
i do not want another deity for you to blame
your fortunes and misfortunes on.
if things go right or wrong,
you should be pointing at yourself.
the point is to use critical thinking, to know how to think
not what to think; there is enough of that already.
be self -aware.
be detached but still participate.
this book is a mirror.
it means whatever you'd like it to mean because
in your own way you're right.
rather than a reflection of your thoughts,
it becomes a reflection of yourself, whoever that may be.
again, i am not here to advocate
any form of religion or belief system.
i am simply sharing my thoughts that i enjoy,
for you to as well.

PARADOX

contact information:
email: i.incognito369@gmail.com
instagram: @tongueslie

please leave a review on amazon and share your thoughts

<u>VOL. II COMING THIS FALL 2019</u>

Made in United States
Orlando, FL
15 February 2022

14828049R00140